A Journey Through
THE
WEATHER

Steve Parker

Illustrated by John Haslam

First published in the UK in 2016 by QED Publishing

A catalogue record for this book is available from the British Library.

ISBN 978 1 78493 450 7

Publisher: Maxime Boucknooghe
Art Director: Susi Martin
Editorial Director: Laura Knowles
Production: Nikki Ingram
Consultant: David Hawksett

Originated in Hong Kong by
Cypress Colours (HK) Ltd
Printed and bound in China by Toppan Leefung Printing Ltd.
10 9 8 7 6 5 4 3 2 1   16 17 18 19 20

Contents

What's the weather today?

What will you wear today? T-shirt and shorts? A raincoat and boots? Or a hat and scarf? If you're planning to go outside, you will need to know what the weather is doing.

If the Sun is shining, you could take a beachball. If the wind is blowing, you could take a kite. If the rain is falling, perhaps you'll need an umbrella.

But the weather can change
in a few minutes.

Watch out for thunderstorms.
If you hear the rumble of thunder then
quickly get inside. Just to be safe,
perhaps you should take everything!

The weather is changing, day and night.

Here comes the Sun

The Earth takes 24 hours to spin around in a circle. During this time, the Sun shines on different places at different times, giving day and night.

Each day begins at sunrise, when the part of Earth where you live turns to face the mighty Sun.

As the world continues to turn, the Sun appears to curve upwards into the sky. It is at its highest around midday. In summer its strong rays can cause sunburn. If you go out, you'd better wear a hat and sunscreen.

The world goes on spinning, and the Sun curves downwards. Its heat and light fade. This is called sunset. Of course, the Sun does not go out. Instead it is shining on the other side of the world.

zZZ

Shapes in the sky

Cirrus

Often the Sun is hidden by clouds. They look dry and fluffy, yet really they are wet. A cloud is millions of tiny drops of water or ice, so small and light that they float in the wind.

The highest clouds are called cirrus. They are faint, tufty, white and wispy, like horses' tails. Usually they occur in fine weather.

Altocumulus

Cumulus

Altocumulus are medium-high clouds. They are small, fluffy, white and grey. If you can see them in the sky, the weather is usually good.

Medium-low clouds are cumulus. They are like puffy, cotton-wool heaps with white tops and grey bases. They bring mixed weather, so don't forget your umbrella!

Raining again

Pitter patter! Pitter patter! It's raining again. Nice weather for frogs! Time to put on a waterproof coat or to open your umbrella.

Rain starts when tiny water droplets in a cloud join or clump together. They get bigger and weigh more. Soon they are too heavy to float, so they fall as raindrops.

Tiny, gentle raindrops are known as drizzle. Short periods of rain are called showers. A downpour is when suddenly lots of big raindrops fall. When that happens, people say it's 'raining cats and dogs'!

Rain may be a pain sometimes, but nature needs it. The rainwater soaks into the soil and helps plants grow. It fills ponds and rivers for frogs, fish and other creatures. It even gives us the water we need to drink, cook and wash.

White world

It's not only rain that falls from clouds. Snowflakes are tiny, soft bits of ice that fall from a freezing cloud. Each snowflake is a crystal with a six-sided pattern. Snow covers everything like a white blanket. You can roll it into snowballs and snowmen. When you walk on snow, it softly crunches underfoot.

Sleet is made of slushy raindrops that are partly frozen. It is not as soft as snow, but like snow, it falls in cold weather.

Hailstones are little balls of frozen ice. They begin as raindrops which get blown up and down by strong winds inside a tall cloud. The top of the cloud is so cold, the drops freeze. Finally they are so heavy, they fall as hailstones. Hailstorms can happen any time, summer or winter.

Stormy day

The weather seems fine and settled but then suddenly... a storm! Tall, dark clouds fill the sky, strong winds blow and the rain pours down.

Storms begin when warm air blowing one way meets cold air drifting from another way. As the two mix, big water droplets form and make huge clouds. The clouds billow up high into the sky and roll down near the ground.

cold air

The cloud's swirling raindrops and ice crystals rub against each other and make their own electricity. This electricity flashes through the cloud or down to the ground as a giant spark called lightning. The lightning heats the air so much it makes the loud noise of thunder. BOOM! Time to find safe shelter!

Where the wind blows

At last, wind blows the storm away. But what is wind and why does it happen?

Wind occurs when warm air and cool air move around. Heat from the Sun makes the ground, water and air warm.

Warm air is light, so it rises. Cool air is heavier, so it moves to take the warm air's place. This moving air is what we call wind.

When there is no wind we say the weather is calm. A small amount of slow wind is called a light breeze. A strong breeze blows as fast as you can run.

Even stronger wind can blow leaves off a tree and washing off a line. A strong gale means danger and might blow you over. Storm-force winds do lots of damage. They can blow down trees, fences and even buildings.

Twister terror

Look out, a twister! This is a tornado – a tall, swirling funnel of super-fast winds.

Tornadoes usually form under storm clouds. Cold air sinks from the cloud and meets warm air rising from the ground. The two start to spin around and form a funnel or pipe shape. The tornado blows along with the cloud. Usually after a few minutes it weakens and fades away.

A tornado's base is normally about 100 metres wide.

Some tornadoes are much more fierce. Their winds can reach more than 350 kilometres per hour – three times faster than a car on a motorway. These super-speed winds can lift a car off the ground. The strongest tornadoes uproot trees, blow down buildings and smash everything in their path.

Hurricane force

The weather's biggest disasters are caused by hurricanes and cyclones – vast storms many hundreds of kilometres across. Huge areas of stormy clouds, extreme winds and drenching rain spin around a calm centre called the 'eye'.

These giant storms usually begin over the ocean. The Sun heats the water and turns it into water vapour, which we cannot see. This warm vapour rises into cooler air where it changes back into water drops, making huge clouds.

Other clouds start in the same way, but hurricane clouds are extra-massive and super-swirling. Their tremendous winds cause enormous damage and the rainy downpours bring severe floods. Luckily, big hurricanes don't happen very often.

Floods

Floods are weather disasters caused by too much rain. The rain pours and pours. Puddles get larger and join together. Rivers, lakes, and drains fill up and overflow. The flood water rises and covers enormous areas.

Floods can bring great damage. They wash away soil and plants, cars and lorries, roads, bridges and railway lines. No one can travel. Farm crops are ruined, so people go hungry. Flood water surges into houses and other buildings.

Flooded areas need urgent help, so lots of people lend a hand. Boats and helicopters bring rescuers to save people and animals. Slowly the waters flow away. Gradually the damage is repaired. Thank goodness! Now life can return to normal.

Where's the rain?

A drought is a long time without rain. It usually lasts weeks, sometimes months and even years. Rivers and lakes dry out. The soil cracks as it dries and shrinks. Plants cannot grow. Grass turns brown, trees die and farm crops fail.

People struggle in a drought. There is not enough water to drink, wash, cook or give to farm animals. Every drop needs saving.

Cars and trucks can bring water in large tanks.

There are ways to help. A hole called a well can be dug deep into the ground, where there is nearly always water. This water is raised by buckets or a pump.

At last, rain falls again and the drought is over.

Why the seasons change

Summer or winter, hot or cold –
throughout the year, Earth's
weather is always changing.
But why does this happen?

The Earth spins around
and around, but it is not
straight up and down.
Instead, it is tilted! This
is what causes the
seasons. As well as
spinning on itself,
the Earth also travels
around the Sun.

Autumn in
the North

Spring in
the South

Winter in
the North

Summer in
the South

The time it takes for Earth to go around the Sun is called a year.

Summer in
the North

Winter in
the South

When the Earth's northern half
is tilted towards the Sun, it
receives more direct warmth
and light. It is summer here.
The southern half leans away
and has winter.

Spring in
the North

Autumn in
the South

As the Earth continues
on its journey, the
northern half begins to tilt
away from the Sun. This
brings autumn and then
winter. The southern half has
spring and then summer... and
so on, year after year.

Sun, no Sun

At the top of the world is the North Pole, and at the bottom is the South Pole. Around them are the polar regions: the Arctic in the north and the Antarctic in the south.

During the few weeks of Arctic summer, the Sun never rises high in the sky – yet it never sets. It is almost warm. Polar plants grow and animals feed on them. But not many, and not for long.

At the same time in the Antarctic, it is deep dark winter. For a few weeks, the Sun never rises. It is three times colder than a home freezer. Plants stop growing and creatures hide away.

Half a year later, it is winter in the Arctic and summer in the Antarctic. In both places, such extreme weather means it is very difficult to survive.

Hot all year

Around the middle of the Earth is the Equator. The Sun here rises high in the sky all through the year, giving lots of heat. Daylight and darkness are about the same length every day. These lands are the Tropics.

Some tropical places have little cloud and rain through the year. These are deserts, with few plants and animals. They may be rocky or sandy, but they are all dry.

Some tropical regions are dry for much of the year, and often have droughts. But then along comes the rainy season when it rains a lot. The rainy season can last for several months.

Some areas in the Tropics have lots of cloud and rain most of the year. Here grow rainforests, with more animals and plants than anywhere else on Earth.

Not too hot, not too cold

Temperate lands are part way between the Tropics around the middle of the Earth and the Poles at the top and bottom. They have four seasons each year: spring, summer, autumn and winter.

Spring days get brighter, warmer and longer, as dark nights become shorter. Nature wakes up. Flowers grow, tree leaves and blossom come out, and birds make nests.

Summer is warm, even hot, with few clouds and little rain. Flowers bloom, bees buzz, butterflies flutter and baby birds grow up.

Autumn days become shorter and cooler, as night time gets longer. Trees lose their leaves in the wind. Bees and other bugs hide. Some birds fly away.

Winter days are short, cold and often gloomy, with strong winds and heavy rain. We need warm clothes. Ponds may freeze as snow covers the ground. Birds and other animals struggle to survive.

Soon it's spring again...

Measure the weather

What's the weather going to be like tomorrow or the day after? To predict or forecast weather, experts measure it every day – in fact, lots of times every day.

Hot, warm, cool or cold? This is called temperature. It is measured in degrees Celsius using a thermometer. Freezing weather is 0 degrees Celsius. Comfortable weather is 20–25. Hot is over 30.

How much rain? Rainfall is measured in millimetres using a rain gauge. A small shower is 1 or 2 millimetres. A day's heavy rain is over 25.

For the latest weather, keep an eye on the sky.

What about wind? Its direction is shown by a weather vane. For example, a north wind comes from the north and blows to the south. Wind speed is measured in miles per hour by an anemometer. A gentle breeze is 5 miles per hour and a gale is 40 or more.

Weather everywhere

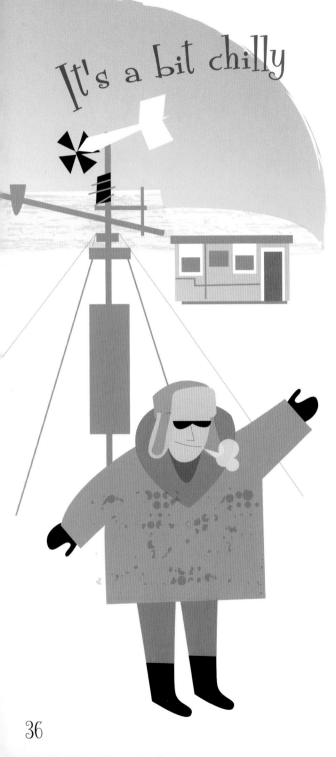

It's a bit chilly

Weather is measured all over the world in many different ways.

On land, places called weather stations take many measurements daily. They send their results by radio, like a mobile phone, to the weather centre. Most work on their own. An expert visits now and then to check all is well.

At sea, ships of all kinds have their own weather stations. There are also weather ships and much smaller weather buoys. These work on their own, all day, every day, and also send their results by radio.

Not a cloud in the sky!

In the air, many planes check the weather as they fly along. Weather balloons measure temperature, wind, and clouds and send the results by radio. The balloon goes up and up until it bursts, then the measuring gadgets float down on a parachute.

It's a bit choppy

What's the forecast?

A weather forecast shows what the weather will be like – probably – in the next hours, days, even a week. To do this, experts use measurements from weather land stations, buoys and balloons.

Weather satellites even send information from high in space. They take thousands of pictures and measurements every day. Some can measure the height of waves on the sea to the nearest 20 millimetres.

All these measurements are put into some of the world's most powerful computers. Experts go through the results and work out the forecasts. These are put on television and radio, in the newspapers, on the internet and mobile phones.

Knowing the weather

Knowing about the weather is so important. It's not just so you can plan when to have a barbeque or visit the beach. Knowing the weather can be as serious as life or death!

Should the farmer harvest his field of wheat? Left for a few days, the wheat will grow even more. But sudden heavy rain could ruin it.

Should this plane take off? The pilots need to know the weather on their journey, in case of a thunderstorm or even a hurricane.

Should this lorry driver set off on his long journey? He must watch out for weather warnings about gale-force winds. These could blow his lorry over.

Should these climbers try to reach the mountain top? It might be fine and calm at the moment. But a huge snowstorm, called a blizzard, could put their lives in danger.

Weather in the future

Weather is what happens now, tomorrow and in the next few days. The overall, general pattern of weather, over many many years, is called climate. Rainforests around the middle of the world have a tropical wet climate. At the South Pole is a polar dry climate. In between are temperate climates.

Climates are changing because the world is gradually heating up. This is known as global warming. It is due to burning of all kinds, such as petrol and diesel in vehicles, and coal, oil and gas in factories, power stations and home heating.

Global warming and climate change may mean more storms, floods, droughts and other extreme weather. One way to slow this is to use energy that does not involve burning and will not run out, such as solar power, wind turbines and hydroelectricity from rivers, waves and tides.

43

Can you spot these weather types?

Can you work out what they are?

Quiz time!

Can you answer these questions about the weather? Here's a hint – you can find all the answers in this book.

1. What is a cloud made from?

2. At what time of day is the sun at its highest?

3. What do you call a hole dug into the ground where there is always water?

4. When does a storm begin?

5. What is the calm centre of a hurricane called?

6. How long does the Earth take to spin around in a circle?

7. What is the area around the middle of the Earth called?

8. What temperature is freezing weather?